CRIMEBUSTERS
DRUG
TRAFFICKING

JILLIAN POWELL

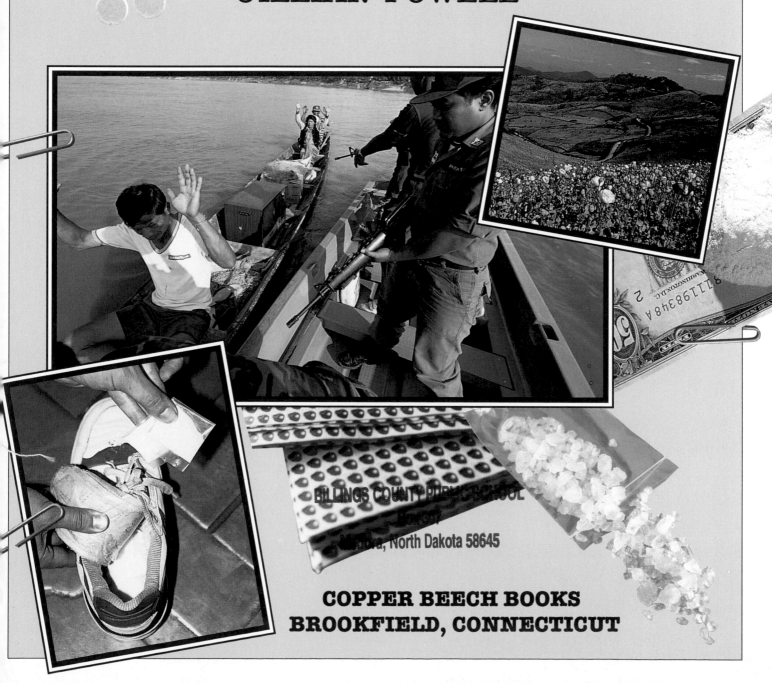

COPPER BEECH BOOKS
BROOKFIELD, CONNECTICUT

© Aladdin Books Ltd 1997

Designed and produced by
Aladdin Books Ltd
28 Percy Street
London W1P 0LD

*First published in
the United States in 1997 by*
Copper Beech Books,
an imprint of
The Millbrook Press
2 Old New Milford Road
Brookfield, Connecticut
06804

Editor Sarah Levete
Consultant
Ian Kille, HM Customs, Drug
Enforcement Team
Design
David West Children's Book Design
Designer Flick Killerby
Picture Research
Brooks Krikler Research
Illustrators
David Burroughs, Flick Killerby

Printed in Belgium

Library of Congress Cataloging-in-
Publication Data
Powell, Jillian.
Drug trafficking / Jillian Powell ;
illustrated by Rob Shone, Flick Killerby.
p. cm. -- (Crimebusters)
Includes index.
Summary: Uses the hypothetical
investigation of an international drug
smuggling ring to examine the work and
cooperation of police forces around the
world in tackling the problems of drug
trafficking.
ISBN 0-7613-0555-6
1. Drug traffic--Juvenile literature.
2. Narcotics and crime--Juvenile literature.
[1. Drug traffic. 2. Narcotics, Control of.]
I. Shone, Rob, ill. II. Killerby, Flick, ill.
III. Title. IV. Series.
HV5809.5.P68 1997   96-35192
364.1'77'0973--dc20   CIP AC

Picture credits
(t-top, m-middle, b-bottom, r-right, l-left)
*Cover bl & br, 1m & bl, 4 all, 5 all, 9t, m & br,
10m & b, 11 all, 12 all, 13 all, 14mr & b, 15t &
m, 16br, 17 all, 18b, 19 all, 21t & bl, 22t, 23 all,
24b, 25 all, 26b, 27m & b, 28t, 29tl, 30 all &
31t – Frank Spooner Pictures; cover mr, 1br, 6t,
8, 9bl, 10t, 14t & ml, 15b, 18m, 20t, 21br, 22b,
24ml, 26t, 28b, 29tr, ml & mr & 31b – Roger
Vlitos; 6bl & br, 7tl, m & b – Mary Evans
Picture Library; 7tr – Hulton Getty Collection;
16bl – Trip Picture Library; 24mr – Topham
Picture Point.*

CONTENTS

INTRODUCTION

"A Worldwide Problem"

Smuggling is an ancient crime. Throughout history, smugglers have tried to avoid customs duties and make money by smuggling goods including salt, silks, wool, tea, coffee, drugs, and arms.

Today's rise in illegal drug use in the West has made drug trafficking – transporting such drugs from one country to another – big business. Drug barons who control the drug trade, from production to trafficking, make huge profits. At the other end of the drug chain, there is an increasing number of drug related crimes, and deaths caused by drug abuse.

Customs organizations report record seizures of illegal drugs, but despite their efforts, they represent only a fraction of the drugs being smuggled.

This book looks at the methods used to traffic drugs. It examines the role of the organizations, such as governments, Customs, police services, and forensic scientists, who work together to fight the problem worldwide. It shows the technology that they use to detect drugs and to follow the trail of the traffickers.

CASE STUDY

CREEPERS

Grappling hooks known as "creepers" were once used by Customs officers to find goods deliberately thrown overboard by smugglers. Officers in row boats dragged the hooks along the seabed to discover casks of brandy, tea, and other smuggled goods, hidden underwater.

CRIMEBUSTING TEAMS

In addition to other duties, Customs organizations are responsible for preventing and detecting drug trafficking – the illegal import and export of controlled drugs (drugs which are either illegal or whose production and availability is strictly regulated). Uniformed and undercover Customs officers have extensive powers: They watch ports and airports, and can search, at random, individuals, baggage, and vehicles. Surveillance vessels and aircraft watch the coastline. Specially trained investigators work behind the scenes, gathering information. Research and development teams test and develop equipment such as underwater robots, to help Customs operations.

The Coastguard
In the nineteenth century, anti-smuggling teams, armed with lanterns and pistols, watched the coastline. Today, coastal surveillance teams use communications systems, and surveillance planes and helicopters to track ships which are bringing illegal cargo ashore.

Forensic Scientists
These experts analyze suspect substances, and identify drugs using chemical tests. They can detect traces of drugs on clothing or on currency. Their findings may be used as evidence in court for the prosecution of traffickers.

U.S. CUSTOMS SERVICE ROVER TEAM MIAMI

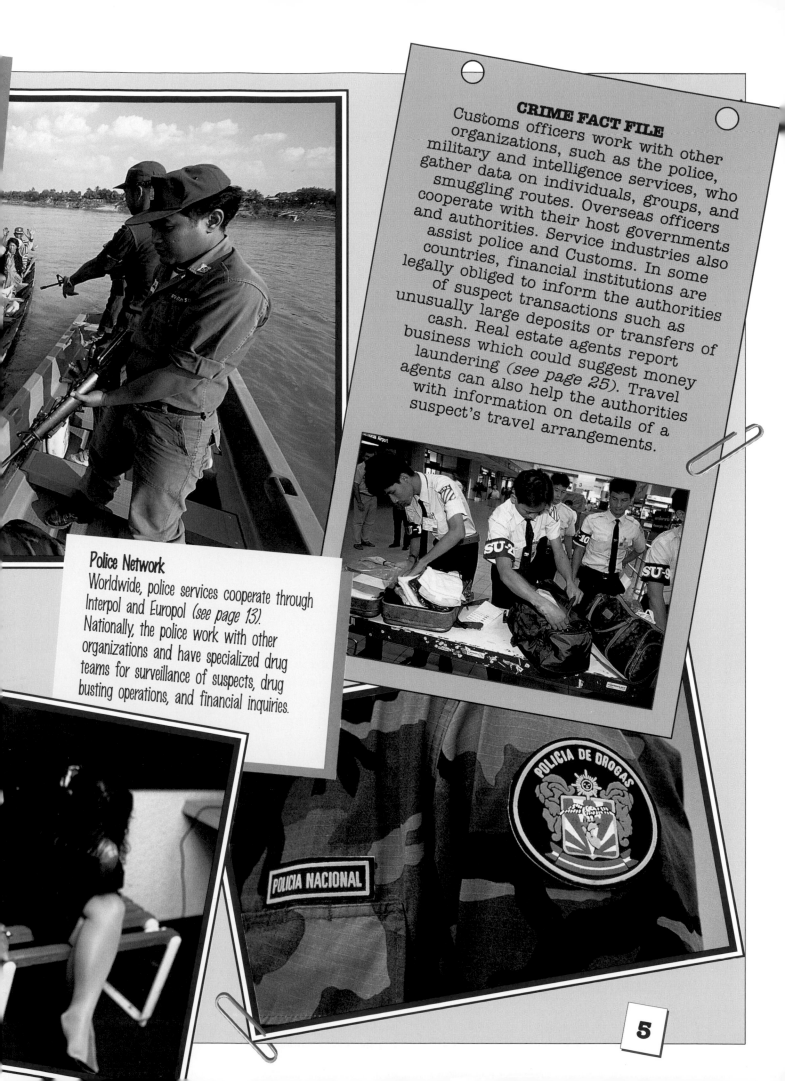

Customs officers work with other organizations, such as the police, military and intelligence services, who gather data on individuals, groups, and smuggling routes. Overseas officers cooperate with their host governments and authorities. Service industries also assist police and Customs. In some countries, financial institutions are legally obliged to inform the authorities of suspect transactions such as unusually large deposits or transfers of cash. Real estate agents report business which could suggest money laundering (see page 25). Travel agents can also help the authorities with information on details of a suspect's travel arrangements.

Police Network

Worldwide, police services cooperate through Interpol and Europol (see page 13). Nationally, the police work with other organizations and have specialized drug teams for surveillance of suspects, drug busting operations, and financial inquiries.

CUSTOMS ALERT

It was a grey February evening. A weary Customs officer on duty at New York's JFK International Airport was nearly at the end of his shift. His thoughts were interrupted by a telephone tip-off. A passenger due to fly to Paris was suspected of trafficking drugs. Quickly, the officer alerted plainclothes officers, who kept

watch for the man. In the crowds, they spotted a man fitting the description given, hurrying to check in. When he had done this, the officers made their way to the sorting area, where baggage is put on to the correct flight.

TOBACCO

Tobacco is a plant whose leaves are used mostly in making cigarettes and cigars. Native Americans smoked tobacco in pipes long before Christopher Columbus brought tobacco

seeds back to Europe from the West Indies in the 1490s. At first, tobacco was used as a medicine to help people relax. In the 1600s, it became fashionable to smoke tobacco. Some inns even provided pipes for customers to use. But not everyone was quick to catch on; above, Sir Walter Raleigh (1552-1618) is shown smoking, but his servant thinks he is on fire!

Today, the taxes from tobacco are an important source of income for many governments. Some people try to smuggle tobacco into a country, without paying the required duty or taxes (see page 7).

...ALCOHOL...

In 1920, alcohol was banned in the United States by a law called Prohibition. Ships arriving in America had to be "dry," sometimes with all alcohol thrown overboard (below). Many people ignored Prohibition, which lasted until 1933: They brewed their own beer, wine, and spirits or bought it in

illegal bars – "speakeasies." Networks of "bootleggers" (illegal makers and smugglers of alcohol) fought each other for control of the profitable market.
Today, many countries prohibit the use of alcohol by minors. Alcohol is forbidden in most Islamic countries, where there may be strict punishments for selling or drinking it.

GEOFFREY CHAUCER

Most famous as the author of *The Canterbury Tales*, Geoffrey Chaucer (1342-1400) was also a Customs officer in England. His formal title was "Comptroller of the Customs and Subsidy of Wools, Skins, and Tanned Hides" in the Port of London, England, from 1374-1386. Chaucer's work would have involved checking the duties paid on goods such as wine and wool as ships entered the Port of London. Political changes after the death of Edward III led Chaucer to lose office, and in the 1390s he wrote *The Canterbury Tales*.

CASE STUDY

Legal or illegal?

For some time, people were unaware of the dangers of addiction to drugs such as morphine, made from the opium poppy, which were available for medicinal and recreational use (right). Until 1904, cocaine was a key ingredient of Coca Cola. Today, some drugs, including morphine, may be produced and manufactured legally under strict conditions for medicinal use, and are available by prescription only. Traffickers deal in stolen or illegally produced drugs which are often dangerous and addictive for the user.

Opium War

The Ancient Sumerians called the opium poppy (far left) "the plant of joy," and used opium to relieve pain and help sleep.
In the nineteenth century, British merchants smuggled Indian opium to China, where it was smoked in opium dens (left). The Chinese Emperor tried to stop this illegal trade by arresting dealers at the Port of Canton (now Guangzhou) and seizing 20,000 chests of opium from British merchants. The Opium War then broke out between China and Great Britain, ending with the Treaty of Nanjing in 1842.

CRIME FACT FILE
Customs are duties or taxes paid to a nation's government on items, such as tobacco or alcohol, that people bring in from another country. Each country has its own laws on this and on which goods are prohibited (not allowed) in the country.

7

The officers examined the suspect's briefcase. Nothing out of the ordinary, but a tip-off was not to be taken lightly. They made a note of the owner's name – a Mr. Parker – his address and his final destination: Brazil. The officers alerted their colleague at the passport desk. He asked Mr. Parker some routine questions about his destination and business there, but was careful not to arouse Parker's suspicions. If Parker was smuggling drugs, they wanted him to lead them to the people masterminding the gang.

The officer noted Parker's passport number and passed the information to the Customs Investigation Division. Parker took the flight to Paris.

Big Business

Today, traffic in illegal drugs has become a vast international business, second only to the illegal arms trade. It is one of the fastest growing areas of international crime, with a turnover estimated at $500 billion a year. Profits from drug trafficking may be used to finance other criminal activities.

CRIME FACT FILE

Taking illegal drugs can cause:
- Addiction to a drug, or death or illness from taking too much of one drug
- Accidents while under the influence of drugs
- Behavior which can lead to serious and dangerous crimes
- Death from overdose after taking more than one drug at the same time
- Infection from sharing unsterilized injection equipment.

CASE STUDY

DRUG-LADEN DOG

In December 1994, U.S. Customs inspectors at JFK Airport saved the life of an Old English sheepdog, when an X-ray scanner (see page 16) revealed about 5lbs of cocaine surgically implanted inside the emaciated dog's body. Customs inspectors examined the dog, shipped as cargo, and found 10 cocaine-laden condoms surgically implanted into the dog's abdomen.

DRUGS

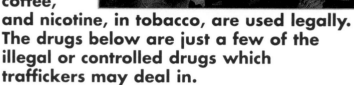

Drugs are substances which affect the mind and or body. Some drugs like caffeine, in tea and coffee, and nicotine, in tobacco, are used legally. The drugs below are just a few of the illegal or controlled drugs which traffickers may deal in.

Cannabis, from the *Cannabis sativa* plant *(bottom right)*, is smoked from the dried leaves (marijuana) or from the resin (hash). It may create a sense of well-being but smoking it may cause lung cancer, and users can come to depend on it. In many countries, it is illegal to possess, sell, or import cannabis.

Cocaine, made from coca plant leaves which grow mainly in South America, speeds up the nervous system, bringing a "high" or buzz. Cocaine may be sniffed *(right)* or injected, or smoked or inhaled as crystals called "crack." The effects can wear off quickly, leaving feelings of panic and anxiety, addiction and depression. It is illegal to manufacture, possess, or import in most countries.

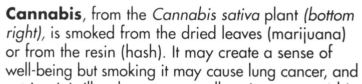

Ecstasy (MDMA or "ADAM") is manufactured as tablets or capsules. The drug gives a high but can cause fits, heart problems, and sometimes death. It is illegal to possess, sell, or import.

Heroin is made from morphine, the active chemical ingredient in opium which comes from the "sleeping poppy" *or Papaver somniferum (top left)*, mainly grown in Southeast Asia and Mexico. Heroin is sniffed, injected, or smoked *(top right)*, and unknown to the user, it is sometimes mixed with chalk, sugar, or brick dust. Heroin is highly addictive, resulting in severe withdrawal symptoms, such as cramps, fever, and shivering. Morphine may be manufactured legally in medicine *(see page 7)*, but it is illegal to manufacture, import, or possess heroin.

LSD (Acid) is produced from chemicals. It takes the form of small pills or tablets of colored paper. The drug is a hallucinogen, which means that it changes the way that users see and hear things. It can cause strange visions and recurring nightmares. The possession, sale, or importation of LSD is illegal in most countries.

Parker's Case

As soon as Parker had been suspected, an investigation team, specializing in targeting drug traffickers, was assigned to the case. They began to make inquiries with their colleagues in Brazil, France, and Bolivia. A few weeks later, they received some interesting information from the National Criminal Intelligence Service (NCIS) in Britain. From New York, Parker had flown to Brazil and then later to Bolivia. Here, undercover officers observed him meeting with a group of men who were suspected of dealing in cocaine. The report triggered "Operation Everest." Parker was being watched and tracked.

The Drug Chain

The drug chain begins with farmers in producer countries and ends on the streets with pushers and users. Raw materials such as coca or opium leaves are grown or gathered in the producer country. In basic factories or laboratories these are processed into powder form which is then often "cut" or mixed with other substances such as bleach, to reduce the purity and to boost the market value. Using a highly organized transport system, traffickers smuggle the drugs into another country, where dealers sell large amounts of the drug for profit. Pushers buy smaller amounts and sell them to drug users.

The U.S. military and governments of producer countries try to stop the drug trade at source. Airstrips and laboratories are destroyed: Above, a Bolivian cocaine paste factory is raided by Umopar, the Bolivian anti-narcotics (drugs) force.

MANUEL de DIOS UNANUE

On March 11, 1992, New York City-based journalist Manuel de Dios Unanue was shot dead in a New York restaurant. The contract to kill de Dios was ordered by the Cali Cartel, in retaliation for articles he had written exposing the Cartel's organization and methods, and chronicling the Cartel's defeats.

Fighting the Barons

Aware of the financial importance of drug crops to farmers, governments have tried to introduce crop substitution programs, offering cash rewards to farmers to grow food crops. But in developing countries in South America and Asia, farmers may be able to earn as much as thirty times more by growing drug crops, rather than crops such as wheat, coffee, or rice. They also face pressure from the drug barons. As a result, governments have resorted to destroying the fields, sometimes by spraying the crops with powerful chemicals *(above)*. However, "armies" try to protect the plantations and the farmers. The drug barons who run the drug cartels (networks) will not give up easily. They are ruthless people, employing growers, manufacturers, packers, shippers, and sellers who become dependent on them for safety, drugs, or financial security.

Aerial surveillance, using planes and helicopters and satellite monitoring, can help to identify areas of drug crop cultivation, such as the "Golden Triangle," an area on the borders between Myanmar (formerly Burma) and Thailand, *(above)*. However, crops such as coca, opium poppies, and cannabis are difficult to detect and may be disguised by surrounding food crops.

Opium poppies for heroin grow on difficult terrain with little water and no fertilizer. Coca leaves for cocaine can be harvested up to six times a year; but these drug crops can leave land unfit for growing other crops.

LUIS CARLOS GALAN

In 1989, the drug barons of Medellín (an area in Colombia) organized the assassination of the Presidential candidate, Luis Carlos Galan, who was a leading opponent of the cocaine trade. The assassination shocked the Colombian government and, with the backing of the United States, they declared "war" on the drug cartels. In the cocaine "war" that followed, hundreds of people were killed.

Parker's Case

The team began to build up a profile of Parker. "NADDIS," the DEA's *(see page 13)* Narcotics and Dangerous Drugs Information System, enabled them to access millions of criminal records: Their suspect did have a previous criminal record for drug offenses. As a student, he had been charged with dealing in cannabis resin. More seriously, he had served a three-year sentence for attempting to smuggle heroin into Canada. Colleagues in the NCIS *(see page 13)*, hopeful that Parker would lead them to bust a major drug chain, gave the team information on Parker's South American contacts.

Global Battle

Intelligence on drug trafficking is gathered by international organizations such as Interpol and the DEA, and by the military, police, Customs, and other agencies. These organizations liaise through computer systems linked worldwide, which are able to translate information as it is sent, so that a report filed in Spanish in Bolivia will be received in English in the United States. Without such cooperation, there would be little hope of tracking and convicting drug traffickers.

Crime Fact File

CODED OPERATIONS
Intelligence operations are code named for secrecy. The names are made up by the investigation team. "Operation Eclectic," led by investigative teams in the United States and Britain, resulted in the arrest of Howard Marks, a leading cannabis trafficker.

Going Undercover

Undercover police officers may pose as drug traffickers or users to discover links in a drug chain. They may approach a dealer and set up a bogus deal, in a "buy and bust" operation. The work can be very dangerous if their identity is discovered by the drug gang. They may have to maintain the pretense, even to other colleagues *(right)*. Drug intelligence officers work undercover with informants, who may be "insiders," giving information in return for rewards.

INTERPOL (the International Criminal Police Organization) holds millions of records of international criminals *(below)* and circulates these worldwide via a vast telecommunications network. A specialist wing focuses on drug trafficking and dealing, money laundering, international routes, and smuggling methods.

EUROPOL (the European Police Office) has a drug unit which works with Interpol and drug liaison officers from European member states, gathering intelligence on drug trafficking and money laundering *(see page 25)* within the European Union.

Heads of Interpol

DEA (Drug Enforcement Administration) is part of the Justice Department, gathering intelligence on drug production and trafficking, and advising and training anti-drug forces.

NCIS (National Criminal Intelligence Service, Britain) collects, analyzes and distributes intelligence on major criminals, including drug traffickers.

Asking Questions

Suppliers of chemicals used in the manufacture of drugs check their records for unusually large cash sales or export orders to developing countries. Information on suspicious activity is passed to intelligence organizations for investigation.

Case Study

Even with vast intelligence networks, the power and influence wielded by drug barons makes them notoriously difficult to arrest and convict. A massive manhunt was organized to capture the chief of the powerful Medellín cartel in Colombia, Pablo Escobar, on whom Interpol has a huge file *(above)*. The cartel fought back with car bombings and killings and by blowing up an aircraft, killing eleven passengers and crew. Another key head of the Medellín cartel, Jorge Luis Ocha, was captured in November 1987, only to be released weeks later by a Colombian judge.

When Parker returned to New York from Bolivia, the investigation team mounted a surveillance operation on him to track his movements. Using mobile units in disguised vans, officers watched Parker 24 hours a day. Hidden from view, a video camera was set up outside his house to record his meetings. Wherever he went, Parker was followed. He was photographed meeting known street dealers and exchanging envelopes and packages with them. Gradually, the team was piecing together the links in Parker's drug chain.

RADAR

Radar (**ra**dio **d**etection **a**nd **r**anging) is an electronic system used to detect and locate moving or fixed objects. A transmitter sends out radio wave pulses which are reflected or bounced back from moving or stationary objects and are picked up by a receiver. The object's precise location can be calculated from the direction of the reflected waves and the time it takes for them to return. Radar was first used in 1925, by scientists Gregory Breit and Merle A. Tuve. By World War II (1939-1945) it was widely used to help track enemy aircraft. Large rotating dish aerials (above right) are used to search the skies for aircraft. Radar equipment may also be compact, fitting into suitcases (left) but still able to locate any activity or movement, whatever the weather conditions or visibility. Radar is ideal for the military or authorities to track ships and aircraft that are suspected of smuggling drugs.

EYE SPY

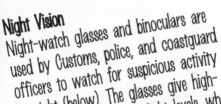

To follow the trail from a drug trafficker or dealer to the people who run the drug gang, the police or Customs must watch and listen...

Telephone wire tapping is used to monitor a suspect's calls. Some taps can be triggered by a change in the shadow cast across the telephone when the handset is lifted. A secret extension line runs between the central exchange and a police listening post, allowing conversations to be monitored and recorded.

Bugs are listening devices used to eavesdrop on conversations in homes, offices, and cars – they may be so tiny that they can fit into a book or pen top.

Cameras, such as the Vulcan 2 (right) can be hidden from view but relay complete images (above).

Night Vision

Night-watch glasses and binoculars are used by Customs, police, and coastguard officers to watch for suspicious activity at night (below). The glasses give high-definition images at low light levels, when smugglers tend to move their cargo.

"ZORRO II"

In 1996, the use of more than 90 court-authorized wiretaps in the Mexican cocaine-busting operation "Zorro II" was credited in dismantling the Mexican organizations that owned and distributed the drug in the United States.

CRIME FACT FILE

Helicopters use high definition thermal imaging systems to follow suspects. A camera picks up heat sources of 98.6°F (the human body) from up to 3,000 ft high, and 2 miles away. Pictures are sent to screens in the cockpit, and then to ground control.

CASE STUDY

15

BORDER CONTROLS

Back at the office, the team had been examining air passenger lists. On Friday, April 13, Parker was booked on a flight to Mexico, with a connecting flight to San Francisco. At last, Friday arrived. When Parker checked in, officers pulled his bags out of the sorting area. They examined them and marked under the lining of the bags with their initials, and photographed them. The bags, now easy for them to identify, were loaded onto the plane, as if nothing had happened.

"Los Extraditables" — "Wanted for Arrest"
Extradition treaties mean that a suspect can be sent across an international boundary, to be brought to trial for crimes committed in that country. The Colombian government wants to bring leaders of the Cali and Medellin cartels — "Los Extraditables" — to the U.S. for trial.

NEW BORDERS, NEW PROBLEMS

Some countries are used to dealing with the problem of drug trafficking. They have sophisticated systems and operations to try and prevent drugs from entering the country (below). However, recent political changes have led to freer movement of people and goods in several Eastern European countries, such as Poland and the Czech Republic (above right). Traffickers have been quick to take advantage of these new smuggling routes. The authorities are working to establish methods of monitoring their borders more effectively.

BAGS, BAGS, BAGS

Checks are made on baggage as it leaves and enters different countries. Before passengers board an aircraft, their luggage is passed through an x-ray scanner (below). On arrival in the other country, Customs officers make spot checks on people coming through with "nothing to declare." Undercover officers watch for passengers acting suspiciously. Rummage crews search baggage holds or sorting areas, looking for signs of uneven packing, and the smell of the glue used to seal hidden compartments.

MIRROR CHECKS

Officers use mirrors with fluorescent lighting to look under vehicles disembarking from ferries. Attached to handcarts, the mirrors can be wheeled underneath vehicles for inspection.

OPEN SEAS

It is even more difficult to police the open seas than it is to monitor border crossings on land.
Ships can carry large cargoes and anchor off remote shores. Smaller boats are then used to ferry the cargo ashore. Much of the cocaine entering Europe via Spain and Portugal is landed in this way, despite the efforts of the coastguard and Customs. At ferry ports, computers are programmed to recognize target vehicles, or profiles of "suspect types." License plate readers check the license plates of vehicles as they disembark, matching them against data stored on the computer. There are thousands of miles of deserted coastline to be patrolled – a massive task for the U. S. Coast Guard and Customs.

Anti-Drugs Alliance

Set up by British Customs to fight drug smuggling and to protect the free-flow of "valid" or legal traffic through borders, this advises ferry operators, cargo handlers, and airline staff on likely signs of smuggling and how to report suspicions to the authorities.

Miami reconnaissance helicopters and boats patrol coastal waters.

THE GOLDEN TRIANGLE

The border regions, the "Golden Triangle" *(see page 11)*, and the "Golden Crescent" (a mountainous area on the border between Afghanistan and Pakistan) are inaccessible, difficult to patrol, and are fertile grounds for opium-growing. Despite frequent raids by the military and frontier police, farmers continue to harvest the crop. The whole operation is controlled by the drug barons whose elaborate networks and armies help protect them from the efforts of the military *(right)*.
In 1983, the Thai Army launched an attack against the biggest drug baron in the Golden Triangle, Khun Sa. Seventeen government soldiers and eighty of Khun Sa's men died. An entire village was destroyed. Khun Sa escaped.

17

Parker's Case

Parker continued his journey to Mexico, but the team was watching.... They felt sure that Parker would use this trip to make contact with the main operators and to bring drugs back into the United States. Colleagues in South America set up surveillance on Parker. In New York, the team could only wait.

At last, their patience paid off. Their man had left

Mexico, stopped off in San Francisco, and was on his way to New York. Officers were alerted. Parker was stopped coming through Customs, carrying his suitcases. Parker was given a routine body search.

Danger Zones

Where it is not possible to use robots or remote visual inspection equipment, Customs officers may have to search inside confined, dangerous places such as fuel tanks and containers. They wear safety harnesses and breathing apparatus, and remain in radio contact with safety and rescue officers outside. They carry alarms which warn of toxic atmospheres. In rusty tanks there may be dangerously low levels of oxygen. Oxygen-enriched air also carries a high risk of fire and explosion.

Sense of Smell

Helping the police and Customs, trained sniffer dogs search for drugs using their sense of smell. The dogs undergo several weeks of training on multi-scent courses with their handlers. "Proactive" dogs are usually gun-dog breeds such as labradors, retrievers, and spaniels. They are trained to sniff out drugs in baggage, aircraft holds, freight sheds, vehicles, ships, and homes. "Passive" dogs are specially trained to sniff drugs hidden on people. They alert their handler by sitting down beside a drug courier, and wagging their tails.

Hidden drugs

Traffickers go to great lengths to hide their stash. They may hide drugs in hollow objects or under fake linings such as the soles of shoes *(above)*. Drugs can be soaked into fabrics, or mixed in liquids and other materials – even food *(below)*. In some cases, heroin is mixed into plaster of Paris and used to make pottery. On one occasion, a man disguised as a priest attempted to smuggle cannabis which had been compressed into the covers of a bible.

However, as traffickers devise more and more devious hiding places, the authorities try to outwit them. Handheld devices called itemizers are now able to detect tiny particles of drugs in the air around clothing or packages.

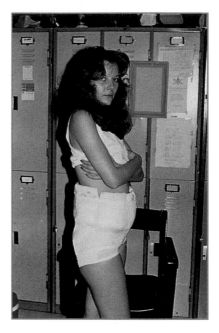

Despite the routine baggage searches and random searches on individuals, drug traffickers continue to try to smuggle drugs through Customs.
Officials, such as cabin crew on an aircraft, will always report suspicious activity which makes them think that a person is smuggling drugs. For instance, couriers *(see page 20)* who are carrying drugs on their body may wear an unusual amount of clothing to disguise their load. Walk-through x-ray machines can "strip-search" passengers, revealing drugs strapped to the body *(above)*. Machines with conveyor belts running through tunnel openings are used to examine parcels and baggage. X-ray vans can also be used as mobile units, hooking up to aircraft holds so that freight can be x-rayed as it is unloaded.

Case Study

SMELLS GOOD

In September 1996, a springer spaniel, Jasper, sniffed out one of the biggest hauls of illicit drugs at London's Heathrow Airport. Jasper was sent to sniff out a jumbo jet after a tip-off from Australia that traffickers were working in the area from which the flight had come. Jasper discovered 397 pounds of cocaine – hidden in a cargo of flowers!

TESTING FOR DRUGS

Parker's Case

Parker's carry-on luggage was opened. Beneath the lining of the bag was a sheet of paper, printed with strawberries. Could this be LSD? The paper was taken away for testing. Meanwhile, Parker was taken to an interview room. The rest of his luggage was opened and searched in great detail. Officers recognized the markings on one of the bags. Carefully concealed in another suitcase, they found plastic-wrapped packages containing white powder. Parker denied all knowledge of the hidden packages.

Case Study

VOLTAIRE
In his novel *Candide*, the French eighteenth century writer Voltaire (1694-1778) wrote about a woman who smuggled diamonds by stuffing them inside her body.

Mules

Couriers or "mules" may carry drugs hidden in their clothing, baggage, or strapped onto their bodies. They may be professional couriers or individuals bribed for a one-stop delivery. Sometimes, traffickers plant their drugs in someone else's luggage or make up an excuse and ask an innocent person to carry their bags through Customs, so it is

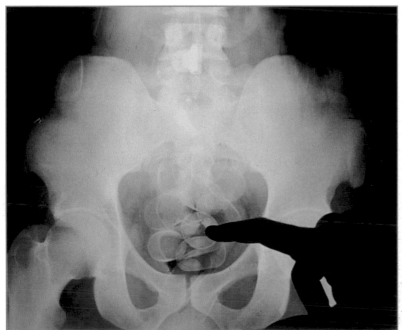

important never to take anyone else's luggage through Customs. Some mules swallow or stuff into their bodies small packages of drugs wrapped in condoms or plastic bags. If a bag bursts, they can overdose and die. If someone is suspected of stuffing or swallowing drugs, two officers of the same sex as the suspect may be authorized to carry out an intimate body search. The suspect may also be required to have a stomach X ray *(left)*. Reported cases include one mule who swallowed 739 capsules of cannabis resin; another swallowed a 9.2-ounce bag of heroin, the size of a pear.

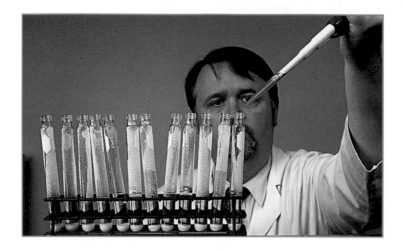

Body Language

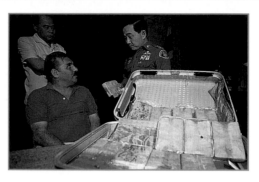

Customs officers are trained to look for signs of anxiety when questioning passengers. Sweaty hands, fast breathing, and a fluttering around the carotid artery below the Adam's apple can betray guilt.

Even when caught "red-handed" *(above)* traffickers sometimes continue to protest their innocence. Officers may apply psychological pressure which may lead the suspect to confess.

Once a suspect has been identified, he or she may be required to undergo intimate body searches to determine the presence of drugs.
Suspect "stuffers and swallowers" may be held in a cell until they need to use the bathroom. A frost cabinet toilet carries waste matter through a glass tube into a metal and glass cabinet where it is caught in bags for examination. Using high-jet water sprays and rubber gloves, officers sort through the waste looking for packages of drugs.

Suspects may be asked to take a urine test using an emit machine. A sample of urine is taken, then measured against control samples which contain a drug element. The test can indicate that drugs are present, either from previous drug use or by being hidden inside the body.

The suspect is sent to the local hospital for any X rays or blood tests *(below).*

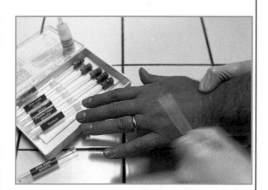

Searching for Evidence

Police entry to suspected dealers' houses must be sudden to prevent drugs from being hidden or swallowed. Pipes are disconnected and sealed with plastic bags so drugs cannot be flushed down the toilet. Borescopes or fiberscopes may be used to examine inside pipes and tanks. Dogs are sometimes used to search the property for the scent of drugs.

Any evidence found – even a single strand of hair – will be carefully bagged, and taken back to laboratories where extensive tests will be carried out to identify the presence of illegal drugs. Forensic scientists will study the evidence *(see pages 23 and 27)* and identify samples scientifically.

IDENTIFYING SUBSTANCES

The suspect packages, along with the "strawberry paper," were taken away to be tested, in on-the-spot "field tests."

A sample of the white powder was put onto a filter paper with a chemical solution, which turned blue, a strong indication of cocaine. The packages were weighed: 6.6 pounds of cocaine. Together with the sheets of strawberry paper which had tested positive for LSD, the packages were sent to the lab for official analysis by a forensic team.

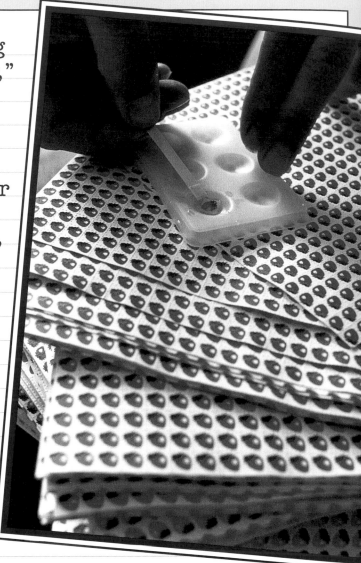

CASE STUDY

A suitcase which was seized at New York's JFK International Airport on a flight from Bolivia was found to contain 38 garments, all of which had been impregnated or saturated with cocaine.

Forensic scientists spent two months analyzing the suitcase and its contents. Eventually, using sophisticated chromatography tests (*see page 23*), they were able to extract and to identify thirteen pounds of cocaine. This had a street value of $1,200,000.

WHAT IS IT?

Suspect substances which are seized by Customs or by the police in raids *(right)*, must be tested thoroughly. Customs officers can carry out on-the-spot field tests to identify the presence of a range of drugs including heroin, cocaine, cannabis, and LSD. Certain chemicals are added to the suspect substance on filter papers or in sealed capsules. Reagents (chemicals which react in a particular or characteristic way when added to other specific substances) produce color-coded results. The results of these tests are allowed as evidence in court, but only as indicators of the presence of drugs.

LOOK CLOSELY

Official confirmation must come from the forensic team *(see pages 26-27).* Here, scientists can identify drugs by chromatography. This separates a substance into a series of simple chemical elements, by passing the mixture through or over a material that slows down the progress of different substances at different rates. This gives a good indication of what a substance is. Further, more detailed tests will complete identification of the substance. Materials which may link the suspect to the location where drugs have been seized are also tested. For instance, fibers are examined under a microscope *(above),* which magnifies even the tiniest object *(see also page 27).*

PRETTY COLORS

LSD *(see page 9)* can be put into absorbent, colorfully decorated paper. To identify LSD, scientists use the Van Urk test. The substance is mixed with a reagent: If LSD is present, the solution turns blue-purple. The substance in the Marquis Test will turn purple if heroin or morphine are present.

"Shake 'n' Vac"

Nicknamed "shake 'n' vac," this forensic test identifies traces of drugs on currency. These can remain trapped in the fibers of the paper but can be shaken out with other dirt. The dust is sprinkled on a sheet of foil and vacuumed into a sealed cartridge. An instrument called a spectrometer is used to separate the chemicals in the sample, and to identify traces of drugs.

Scientists were busy in the forensic labs; colleagues in Mexico were following up the leads Parker had unknowingly given them; the investigation team in New York began to collect more evidence against Parker.

Financial inquiries into Parker's bank accounts showed that he had been regularly depositing large amounts of cash. The timing of these deposits coincided with his trips to Mexico and San Francisco. Was this mere chance? Parker had several bank accounts, showing large amounts of money. Could he have made so much money as a "sales rep," the job he claimed to have?

CRIME FACT FILE
Several laws have been passed worldwide to crack down on money laundering, but this has not stopped drug barons from enjoying their illegally made money, shown by the castle pictured above, home to a Colombian drug baron.

The 1988 Vienna Convention gives investigators access to bank accounts to search for evidence and to make sure that any assets (sources of income, such as a business or savings account) are frozen – preventing the suspect from gaining access to them.

In some countries, banks are legally required to notify the authorities of suspect deals, and the evidence collected can be used in court.

CARD TRICKS

Money launderers try to avoid detection by transferring cash without official documentation or receipts. The receipt for cash may take the form of a playing card torn in half, so that only the two parties involved carry evidence of the transaction. Drug traffickers may open up bank accounts or safe deposit boxes (above) under false names.

MONEY LAUNDERING

Drug barons protect themselves by putting the money from drug deals into what appear to be legitimate concerns. Money laundering is making the proceeds from illegal activities look as if they come from legal businesses. An estimated $50 billion is laundered annually through financial transactions. Cash from drugs may be shipped overseas to countries where there is no financial regulation. It is then put through the system in the account of an offshore company (one which is registered in another country), only to be wired or sent back to a regulated country. Drug money may also be used to buy property, antiques, and jewelry, or invested in legal businesses, with the help – knowing or unknowing – of banks, lawyers, and accountants.

Specialized police teams focus on identifying and seizing proceeds from drug trafficking and tracing the flow of laundered money. Their investigations may lead them to casinos *(above)*, where large amounts of cash often change hands.

CRIME FACT FILE

The BCCI investigations *(below)* led to the arrest of dictator General Manuel Noriega of Panama. In April 1992, he was found guilty of racketeering, drug trafficking, and money laundering. He had accepted bribes from Colombian drug barons in exchange for protecting their cocaine shipments to Florida.

Financing Terror

The huge profits that drug barons make from drug dealing make them very powerful and dangerous.

Drug money may be used to try and bribe corrupt politicians or officials so that they will not catch and convict the drug criminals. There is evidence to suggest that many terrorist groups receive funding from the illegal profits of the drug cartels.

BCCI
CASE STUDY

In 1991, the Bank of Credit and Commerce International (BCCI), based in Abu-Dhabi (part of the Arab Emirates) was convicted of laundering profits from drug trafficking. U.S. investigators codenamed their operation "C-chase" after the slang "C notes" for the $100 bills which the bank was accepting.

BILLINGS COUNTY PUBLIC SCHOOL
BOX 307
Medora, North Dakota 58645

25

Parker's Case

The forensic tests were positive. Parker was held on suspicion of importing controlled drugs. The team obtained a warrant to search his New York apartment. Sniffer dogs found packages of cocaine, more LSD, and a large amount of cash, all of which would be used as evidence against him. The team was delighted. They had broken the first link in a major international chain. They hoped that colleagues abroad would soon be able to arrest the masterminds behind the gang. For the moment, however, "Operation Everest" had stopped at least some illegal drugs from being on the streets.

Case Study

Forensic examination of tiny fibers found in a package of illegal drugs linked it to a rug in a drug dealer's home. Forensic scientists were able to describe exactly to the police, the pattern on the rug from which fibers had come!

Case Study

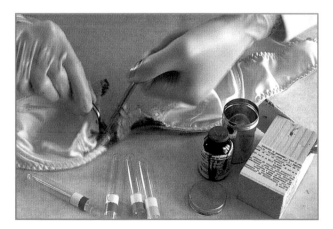

DRUGS MONEY

In January 1996, $427,000 in cash was seized by Customs from the trunk of a car about to board a ferry in Harwich, England. Forensic scientists carried out tests on the car and all the luggage, including clothes *(above)*. Results showed that the money had been contaminated with cocaine.

Testing

Modern forensic science dates back to the mid-nineteenth century. It is the technique of using scientific methods in solving crimes.

Forensic scientists work in police laboratories. They are responsible for explaining in court the significance of their findings: Their evidence is often crucial in securing a conviction in court.

However skilled a drug trafficker may be at covering up his or her tracks, the work of a forensic scientist may be enough to link the criminal to a crime, with only the tiniest of clues.

Hair Tests

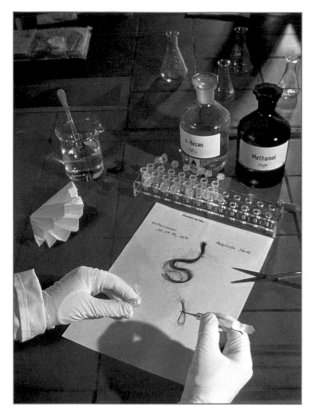

A "DDH" (drug detection in hair) test enables scientists to use strands of hair to detect drugs in the body.

Microscopic examination of a single strand of hair can indicate a person's age and sex. Today, new tests can detect the presence of drugs.

The hair is exposed to various chemicals and substances. Certain chemical reactions will confirm the presence of drugs in the hair.

However, this test cannot determine whether the drug was consumed or if the hair was contaminated (came into contact) with the drug. Forensic scientists must be certain about all the details of their findings. For this reason, the DDH test needs to be more exact in its findings before it is used widely.

Dead or Alive?

Forensics can test for drugs in the long-dead and the living! Scientists have found traces of cocaine and tobacco in Egyptian mummies. But how could the ancient Egyptians have had drugs grown only in continents not discovered until 1,000 years later? Could they have discovered the Americas?

Evidence

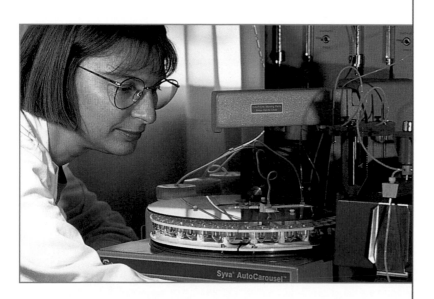

THE TRIAL

The investigation team had gathered evidence against Parker. The officers were able to back up their surveillance reports and video film with forensic evidence, showing that Parker had been involved in illegal trafficking and dealing in cocaine and LSD.

1 Surveillance film showed Parker meeting and exchanging packages and envelopes with known street dealers.

2 A NCIS file reported Parker's meetings in Bolivia with known cocaine dealers.

3 Customs officers were able to provide photographic evidence showing that the bag taken to Mexico by Parker was used to bring back cocaine.

4 Forensic scientists confirmed that the powder carried by Parker had proved positive as cocaine, and that he was also carrying sheets impregnated with LSD.

5 Police were able to testify that drugs had been found in Parker's apartment.

6 Forensic evidence showed that the drugs were cocaine from Mexico, and LSD manufactured in California.

7 Forensic tests proved that cash held in Parker's apartment was contaminated with cocaine.

8 Under questioning, Parker finally admitted to trafficking and possession of cocaine. He also admitted to trafficking and possessing LSD.

The evidence was so strong that Parker pleaded guilty to trafficking in cocaine and LSD. He was convicted. Customs investigators had broken the links in a drug chain that stretched from Mexico to New York. It would not be long before leading members of the chain were arrested.

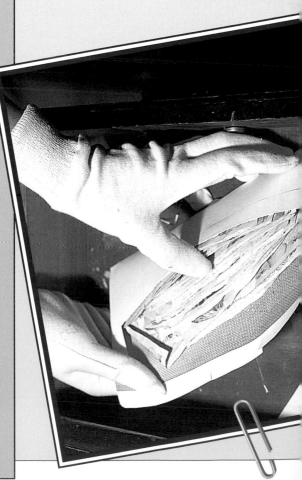

The evidence was enough to convict Parker. However, his sentence was reduced because he told the police about his contacts and the people running the gang. The police were on their trail...

United States

- The cocaine market is worth $15 billion-$17 billion a year.
- 150-175 tons are consumed at a street price of $100 per ounce.

South America

- Colombia's Cali cartel may control more than 70 percent of world cocaine business.
- Peru cultivates 60 percent of world coca, Bolivia 21 percent, and Colombia 8 percent.
- In Bolivia, Colombia, and Peru over a million people are employed in the illegal drug trade.

International smuggling routes

Mexico and the Caribbean

- Jamaica is a major area for the cultivation of cannabis.
- 60 percent of cocaine bought in the U.S. now passes through Mexico.

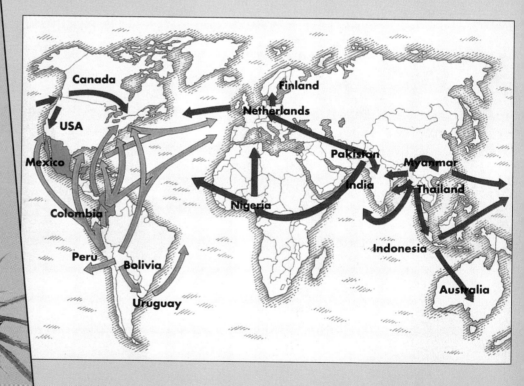

Cocaine
Opiates
Cannabis growth

The major drug trafficking routes cover most of the world.

Europe

Africa

- Nigerian cartels are trying to control heroin trafficking as the country becomes an important "transit" country – a country through which drugs are smuggled to another country.

- The drug, Khat, (left) is grown in East Asia. Today, it is exported legally to many countries but some governments are considering whether to make it illegal.

- Europe is becoming a more attractive target for cocaine traffickers as prices rise above those in the United States, and European Community border controls are reduced.

- A seizure in 1992 of a ton of cocaine on the Finnish border suggests that cartels are trying to establish themselves in Russia.

- Spain has become a main gateway for cocaine entering Europe.

- The Netherlands is the main producer country of "psychotropic" or hallucinogenic drugs such as Ecstasy and LSD.

Asia

- China is now thought to be the second most important route for heroin produced in the "Golden Triangle" (border between Myanmar and Thailand).
- Opium is produced in 15 of China's 22 provinces.
- Afghanistan, Iran, Pakistan, Myanmar, Thailand, and Laos are now all major producer countries of opium.
- New areas for coca growth (cocaine) are being explored in Central Asia.

World Hauls

In 1995, worldwide hauls amounted to:
- 16,609.84 kilos of heroin
- 286,347.39 kilos of cocaine
- 1,277,815 kilos of cannabis
- 3,412.20 kilos of opium
- 138,831 doses of LSD

The annual value of sales in cocaine, heroin, and cannabis in the West is estimated at $122 billion.

The biggest drug haul was seized on October 24, 1996, in Holland where 1,650 lbs of cocaine (worth approximately $112 million) were found concealed inside aluminum ingots consigned from Venezuela.

GLOSSARY

Cartel A group of businesses which control production and distribution.

Courier Someone who takes illegal drugs from one country to another, on behalf of another person.

Duties Taxes which are paid on goods brought from one country to another.

Informant A person who reports on the activities of others.

Intelligence Gathering and interpreting information.

Impregnate To put one substance into another.

"Nothing to declare" The phrase used when people bring into a country only the amount of goods allowed, without needing to pay extra duty.

Opiate Any drug made from or containing opium.

Producer country A country in which drug crops are grown.

Reagent A substance with characteristic reactions, used as a chemical test.

Solvent A substance that dissolves another.

Surveillance Keeping a watch on people or places.

INDEX